Snowflake Chronicles 1

Right thinking on Abortion

Nicola Wright

Connor Court Publishing

THE SNOWFLAKE CHRONICLES

RIGHT THINKING ON
ABORTION

NICOLA WRIGHT

Connor Court Publishing Pty Ltd
PO Box 7257
Redland Bay QLD 4165

sales@connorcourt.com
www.connorcourtpublishing.com.au
Phone 0497 900 685

ISBN: 9781925501964

Front Cover Photo: Canva Content media ID: MACdCXB7E8U
Printed in Australia

Contents

Snowflakes Chronicles 1

Introduction

Roger Franklin

A true story, sad in more ways than I can imagine, not being a woman, and offered for what it's worth. In comparison with the book you're about to read, perhaps not much. Anecdotal and entirely subjective, it's a memory blurred by the opacity of perception, the clouding of what all the academic smarties now call "gender" and which – the theorists are right about this – will never let a man entirely grasp the female mind and motive, even when they are lovers, which we were. She was gorgeous, fun and I adored her, especially what I took for sincerity and honesty. A troubled youth – drugs and St Kilda companions – she'd left all that behind two decades before we met, "got clean", as she would say, "fixed myself". It was that realistic self-appraisal, the candour and self-knowledge that helped her kick the needle, which I recognise in retrospect as one of the magnets that drew me to her, perhaps the greatest of them all early on. She was a woman who knew herself, or so I surmised, and that is powerful attractor.

It was Saturday morning when she spoke of it, pillow talk after the Greek neighbour had taken note of the little hand passing 8, which meant he could exercise his right under local bylaws to play with noisy power tools. For some reason the talk of coffee and which of us should make it slipped into a reminiscence of her former marriage. A less indolent sort than I, it emerged her ex would leap gazelle-like from their bed to brew the pot and brown the toast. And somehow, in the way these things do, one person's memory prompted another's joke.

She was doubly blessed for not having had kids bouncing all over the bed, I said, inspired by memories of my own ruptured marriage's child-rearing days. "Kids in the morning! I'd rather a wog with a bandsaw any day of the week."

I barely heard her reply.

"Almost."

It was very nearly a sigh, uttered so quietly it came as more reflection than response, so I took a second to grasp it was children she was talking about, not a New Australian consorting with a bandsaw. At that point, in her early mid-forties, she was childless and unbothered by it, or so I thought.

"I terminated the pregnancy," she continued, using the euphemism of clinical language you hear so often when abortion is the subject. "We were splitting up, he was into dope and cheating and… " and there a pause "…I just would not have *that* man's baby."

She all but spat the last sentence, and the vehemence of it was shocking. I rose just then to make us brekkie. It seemed a handy moment to be doing something else, for while her ex had been mentioned at other times, never with a such loathing that spoke of passing stern judgment on him and a death sentence on his line and heir. The sins of the father visited upon his unborn child. I recall the smell of toasting bread as I tried to get my mind around what she had just told me. It seemed at first glance to be criminally unfair to have killed a child because his father no longer passed muster. Perhaps, had she been raped… but still, even then, a life extinguished before it could begin for no fault nor crime of its own.

Abortion? A man 'gets' it, sort of. Pro or con, it matters not. Even the most ardent male opinions, those on either and both sides, can be no more than academic when the holder is fated never to know, not even to realistically imagine, what it is like to have a new life blooming between one's hips. Abortion, nasty business. Best not to think too much about it. Their bodies themselves etc., and leave the girls to it. Isn't that the shot, what the equality commissioners are always saying? They know what's best. The comfort of evasion. The false refuge of choosing not to strike and settle on a moral position, especially about what she had just told me.

The subject opened, it emerged in dribs and drabs that she was not quite so sanguine about going childless as I had taken her. There were mentions of fertility drugs and friends who had conceived late and successfully. Just such a couple mentioned over dinner that they had some fertilised and frozen eggs left over, their IV treatments having produced a fine set of twins and that was enough of a family for them. Later that night, again in bed, she wondered if they might gift those dormant eggs to her. We took none of those steps, but nor did we employ any protection. I remarked that, were she to fall pregnant, I wouldn't have a problem with being a fifty-something father. Much as I'd griped in misanthrope mode about a small person in rabbit-ear pyjamas leaping on nightshift worker's testicles at 6am, the fact is that I rather like kids, and by then my own had grown and recently flown. I missed the Auskick stuff and Little Aths, even being called by the principal to 'work on your boy's behaviour'. He had turned out okay, my son, better than I'd anticipated and certainly in excess of his headmaster's expectations. I'd take another turn with the stroller should it happen, which I didn't think it would in light of her age, and I'd do so happily.

Well pregnant she became soon after. The cliché is that expectant mums are "radiant", but she was that and more, lit up not at that early stage by an hormonal flush but by the sheer joy of being pregnant. I'd never known a happier person. What I had taken for cheerful resignation had actually camouflaged a stoic and unspoken yearning to which she would never before had admitted. Now she did. Sometimes, although I said nothing, I thought of the child she aborted and wondered if her bliss reflected a relief at a being granted fertility's clemency.

It was good for a while, wonderful even. When I cooked there were no longer admonitions to go easy on the butter. She was eating for two, of course, and absolutely untroubled by morning sickness. We looked a thousand times at those grainy ultrasound images and tried to figure if a tiny curlicue between foetal legs was a penis or just some graphic distortion. It was really fun, even down to the nuts and bolts of planning. The nursery would be the back room and, yes, we made a note be on the lookout for a nice rocking chair, perfect for breast-feeding. A sister-in-law who was moving house took that opportunity to drop off a box of used baby clothes and there was much laughter and gratitude as romper sets were examined and appraised, accepted or rejected. There was no longer any morning pressure to make the coffee. Along with all alcohol, she banished caffeine as a hazard to the preciousness in her belly. The fine print on packaged food was pored over with a Talmudic eye for detail and downside.

At some point between three months and four months, slow disaster. Her doctor told her the foetal heartbeat was weak and fading. She should reconcile herself to losing it, she was told. At her age these things happened, and this was the greatest comfort the doctor could offer. The foetus died in stages, day by day over the week that followed until there was nothing to be heard at all. There followed a D&C procedure at Royal Melbourne Hospital and I waited for her outside. Barely through the front door at home, she sagged against the wall and slid to the floor sobbing and beyond distraught, knees pulled up beneath her chin. She had wanted a kid for so long, she said in disjointed, anguished syllables, "and now this."

My thoughts as I cradled her on that hallway rug went diplomatically unexpressed. She could have had the child she ached for, who by then would have been all of fourteen, if not for the abortion. As it happened that was her thought too because between the sobs she said as much. The fury directed against the memory of her ex-husband acquired a different aspect. She had killed what she now wanted most of all and someone had to carry the blame. Projection made it him. I held her tighter and said nothing because, well, there was nothing to say. Eventually, when the paroxysm of grief had passed, been drawn back deep inside and paved over, I helped her to her feet and walked her to the bed, where she asked that I pull the curtains and leave her alone in the dark. I still remember how the hallway runner had left the impression of woven seagrass upon a cheek sodden with tears.

We broke up not long after because everything was somehow different after that. There was a distance and a resentment about her, a grief, or so I intuited, that she had hauled back and down after its public airing in that hallway display of absolute misery, buried it as best she was able deep inside.

The feminist texts and "pro-choice" editorials never mention that.

-- Roger Franklin, Editor Quadrant online

Foreword

The Christian position on abortion is well-known. It is the position that, as a Christian pastor, drives my own thinking and writing on the topic. And it is predicated on the belief that God cares for unborn children just as much as he cares for their pregnant mothers. Indeed his abundant care extends to all other mothers, and fathers, and all the people he has made. Of those yet unborn the Psalmist David writes:

O Lord, you have searched me and known me!...you knitted me together in my mother's womb...My frame was not hidden from you, when I was being made in secret...the days that were formed for me, when as yet there was none of them.[1]

There are difficult texts in the Bible, but as an expositor of the Scriptures, this simply is not one of them. And so the Christian position – that abortion is the taking of human life, and therefore wrong – is really quite simple. But for most women – including some that I have had the privilege of meeting and helping – the matter of an unplanned or unwanted pregnancy is anything but simple. Unsurprisingly, many report that it was the most difficult decision they have had to make, and the most stressful and terrifying situation they have ever encountered.

Apart from individual cases, abortion remains complex. Anyone with even a rudimentary knowledge of American politics knows that the way abortion intersects with law, philosophy, religion and medicine makes it an issue unlike any other. And any observer of the Australian political scene will have seen the increasing polarization taking place in this country around the issue. As I said, even as a Christian who believes abortion is wrong, it is not a simple matter.

And so I am thankful for this book, which will prove helpful in a way that my preaching and teaching on David's Psalm cannot.

Women, regardless of their beliefs, deserve accurate, honest, and clear information about pregnancy and abortion. Women in the midst of an unplanned or unwanted pregnancy need this as a matter of priority, and options as a matter of urgency. And all Australians will benefit from the opportunity to think seriously and sensibly about what will become a divisive issue for them, as it already is for politicians, doctors, and nurses (among others).

Nicola Wright is a friend, although hardly a co-religionist in the strict sense. Our common battles have been ideological rather than doctrinal. And in producing this volume my friend has done us all a great service. If you're after a religious treatment of abortion and kindred issues I can recommend two from my Reformed perspective, although there are, no doubt, many more.[2] But this book isn't in that category. In these pages, however, you will find an accurate, honest, and clear account of what abortion is and what it means for society, for women, and for babies. For the sake of expectant mothers, those who love them, and those children yet unborn, I commend this book to you, and trust that it will make clear the dehumanization that attends the scourge of abortion.

-- Chris Ashton, April 2018

1

Why talk about abortion?

Everyone has an opinion on abortion, usually a very strongly held one. Sometimes it appears we keep having the same conversations and the same arguments about it without getting anywhere, and this is probably true. The pro-life and pro-choice camps are deeply entrenched in their viewpoints and it can seem as though nobody is open to taking on board new information or changing their minds.

Abortion is an important and divisive topic and it is for this reason that we must keep talking about it, no matter how futile it can sometimes seem. It is literally a matter of life and death. In the mainstream, abortion is framed as a right, as something that liberates woman from their traditional roles and frees them from unwanted pregnancies and the responsibility that comes with bearing children. Women now have the "choice" and plan their lives accordingly.

Abortion is also presented as a simple procedure that is not a "big deal". Even magazines for teenaged girls talk about abortion as something that is a normal part of life, and yet this ignores the physiological and psychological impacts abortions have on women, impacts that we don't often hear about. Most women don't talk about their abortions or how they feel afterwards, and the topic is often taboo.

Being pro-choice or pro-life is not so much a political issue as a moral one. Despite the rhetoric that paints abortion rights as a positive development, that is embraced by most of the population, the facts tell a very different story. 50% of Americans believe that abortion should be legal in some circumstances, but only 29% think it should be legal in all circumstances (abortion on demand). The population is also fairly split on whether people think of themselves as pro-choice (49%) or pro-life (46%). These percentages have substantially changed from the mid-1990's when 56% of Americans considered themselves pro-choice and compared to only 33% who considered themselves to be pro-life.[3]

People who hold anti-abortion or pro-life views can be found in all walks of life. In addition to the many pro-life people who are religious and conservative, people holding pro-life views can be found amongst feminists, libertarians, atheists, and members of progressive political groups like the Democrats in the US and the Greens.

The pro-life position is often characterised as a matter of religious belief and there is no denying that many anti-abortionists are indeed people of faith. But the most compelling pro-life arguments are not religious in nature and speak to philosophical and scientific truths on the nature of life and humanity.

Perhaps you believe that abortion is a private matter, and that the decision to have an abortion is nobody's business but the mother's. It seems like a reasonable stance. But abortions are about more than the woman's body. They involve a unique new life, vulnerable and reliant on the mother for their continued sustenance, a new life with potential that has a future value to other human beings, that shouldn't be discounted in favour of the preferences of its mother.

Rather than talking about easy access to abortion as an undisputed positive and liberating development, we need to be honest to our young women about the reality of foetal development and abortion procedures. We need to acknowledge why women seek abortions, as well as the often ignored negative psychological and physiological impacts of abortion. We also need to acknowledge that very many women who seek abortions are already cognizant that they are ending a life; they realize that their choice is imperfect and yet a pregnancy is to them intolerable.

We also need to talk about the current legal status of abortion in Australia and whether it adequately balances the needs of the mother, with the rights of unborn children. We need to have conversations about abortion so that we can touch hearts and minds. We need to talk about real alternatives to abortions and how we can do better.

2

Where does life begin?

We all know that we started life in the womb, where we grew and developed to the point that we could survive, with a bit of help, outside of our mother's bodies. But when talking about abortion with people, it becomes apparent that the mechanics of fertilisation and foetal development are not always well understood.

When discussing fertilisation for example, some people will try and equate eggs and sperm cells with a fertilised egg or zygote. Others compare fertilised eggs to "fingernails or hair". The argument goes something along the lines of 'fingernail cells contain DNA, but they are not human beings.' Their point generally is that if their sperm, or their fingernails can be disposed of readily, then so can a zygote.

Others are unaware of how early the developing foetus moves on from being an homogeneous, but rapidly dividing "clump of cells" to into a being with distinct organs, a heartbeat and a nervous system. Without adequate knowledge of the stages of foetal development, it's impossible to form an opinion of abortion that is based on facts.

All the cells in our body, except the sex cells have two sets of chromosomes and are called "diploid" cells. The sex cells, that is, the female ovum and the male spermatozoa are "haploid" cells and have only one set of chromosomes. At the point of conception, the nuclei of the two haploid sex cells are combined and become one diploid cell called a zygote, with a unique genetic composition made up of one set of chromosomes each from the mother and the father. It's at this point that sex is determined based on whether the sperm cell has an X or Y chromosome.

Between fertilisation, which usually occurs in the fallopian tube, and implantation into the wall of the uterus, the zygote begins to divide into multiple cells and is known as the preimplantation conceptus. Some of the cells at this stage will later go onto to develop into the embryo, and some will form extra-embryonic tissues.

During this stage, the cells are acting individually rather than as a one multi-cellular organism. The early embryo of less than eight cells can fuse into another or split and become twins. After travelling down the fallopian tube, the conceptus then implants in the wall of the uterus.

The science of foetal development is clear that a new entity with its own unique DNA is created when the ovum and the sperm combine to form the zygote. There is debate though, about whether the one celled zygote represents a unique individual, as after it starts dividing, some of the resultant cells make up extra-embryonic tissues, which as the name suggests are separate from the embryo. Also, while the embryo is still less than eight cells, it can split to form twins or combine with another early embryo.

As Norman M. Ford carefully argues in his book *When Did I Begin? Conception of the Human Individual in History, Philosophy and Science* there is a case for the embryo not becoming a unique individual until around 15 days after conception, after which the embryo is distinct from the extra-embryonic material and is a worthy human individual.[4] Either way, scientifically speaking, the point at which a new entity is formed is very early.

4 Weeks

When describing the stages of foetal development and pregnancy, the weeks are counted from the woman's last period. Therefore, at four weeks of pregnancy it is approximately two weeks from the time of conception. At this stage, the embryo has implanted into the wall of uterus and the embryo and extra-embryonic tissues are differentiated. Some pregnancy tests are sensitive enough to detect pregnancy at this stage, which is around the time a woman's period would be due.

5 Weeks

By weeks of pregnancy the mother may have noticed that her period is late, and it is at this time that a pregnancy test is typically taken. The embryo is around the size of a sesame seed and already has a neural tube and the beginnings of a circulatory system. Its heart begins beating sometime during the fifth week. The placenta and umbilical cord are already working.

6 Weeks

At six weeks, the embryo has the beginnings of a face, and budding arms and legs. It's heart beats at around 100 - 160 beats per minute.

8 Weeks

At eight weeks, the foetus has the beginnings of fingers, toes and eyelids, and is constantly moving around even though it is too small for the mother to feel it. Neural pathways are rapidly being formed. The foetus is about 40mm long. From conception to 8 weeks, development and growth has been extremely rapid.

10 Weeks

By ten weeks all the vital organs are in place. The foetus kicks, swallows and pulls faces. It has fine hair on its skin and finger nails. The brain is rapidly developing and is disproportionately large compared to the rest of the body.

12 Weeks

By twelve weeks the foetus has developed reflexes and will respond to stimulation. Its kidneys are fully functioning, and the face is recognisably human. The brain continues to rapidly develop. It is roughly the size of a lime. Twelve weeks marks the end of the first trimester.

2nd Trimester

The second trimester of pregnancy is from week thirteen to week 28. By this time, the foetus has fully functioning organs, which continue to grow and develop. During this time, the baby develops its hearing, and can move his or her eyes around. At around twenty weeks the mother begins to detect the movements of her baby, sometimes called "the quickening".

Babies have been observed to be experiencing REM sleep as early as 23 weeks.[5] During week 25 the foetus starts to respond to sounds including the mother's voice. By the end of second trimester the baby weights around 800 grams. The earliest surviving premature baby was born at 21 weeks and 5 days.[6]

3rd Trimester

During the last trimester of pregnancy, the baby's organs continue to mature, and the baby continues to grow. Research into foetal behaviour reveals that foetuses selectively respond to external stimuli earlier than previously thought, and that they regulate their responses to the stimuli through actions such as yawning, crossing their arms and touching themselves.[7] MRI studies have also shown that the neural networks that enable consciousness are present in the foetal brain.[8]

It's clear that the embryo develops very quickly from early after conception. By three weeks after conception the heart is already beating, and the senses are developing in even in the first trimester. The later foetus also interacts with the outside environment, recognising sounds and shapes. While the foetus is in utero the human experience has already begun.

Look on any pregnancy support website that outlines foetal development and you will see the embryo and foetus referred to as a "baby", and its developmental stages described in loving detail. But when the foetus is unwanted by the mother, it is no longer referred to as a baby, but rather as just a "clump of cells".

Abortion and philosophy

In the abortion debate pinpointing when life begins is central. If you believe that life begins at conception, then you are more likely to be anti-abortion. Many people who defend abortion either reject that an embryo or foetus is a human life or change the meaning of human life so that a developing foetus does not qualify, or both. To do so, the point at which life begins becomes less of a matter of science and more one of philosophy.

Pro-choice people will often argue that even science does not know the point at which a zygote or embryo becomes a "new life". Of course, they do not dispute that a zygote or embryo is alive, only that science doesn't know at what point it represents "human life".

Embryology has told us for at least 30 years that conception is the point at which a unique organism comes into being with its own genetic code, but this is often dismissed as irrelevant to the abortion debate.[9] The developing human starts as just a "clump of cells", yet to form any recognisably human characteristics and is developing along a continuum from conception up until birth, upon which any point can be arbitrarily assigned as the moment when a valued and viable human existence can be said to have started.

The obvious problem with such arbitrary assignations is the timing of this magical moment, which differs according to personal beliefs. For some it is at the point that the foetus can feel pain, for others is when brain activity is detected. Some like to pick weeks of development, such as 8 weeks or 22 weeks, others think that birth marks the start of a human existence. Just the attitude of the mother is enough of a deciding factor for some people: if the mother is happy to be pregnant, then the foetus is human life worthy of protection, if the mother is unhappy about her pregnancy no matter at what stage, the foetus has no rights, and can be dispensed with.

Some people, contrary to scientific evidence, have the most obtuse beliefs about the developmental status of a foetus. They believe that a foetus doesn't have any meaningful brain activity in utero including reactions to stimuli until birth, at which point it miraculously began interacting with the outside world, this despite scientific evidence to the contrary which shoes that the human foetus interacts with stimuli in the womb.

Many pro-abortionists base their abortion views on rights. They have no argument with the fact that a foetus is "alive" or can be considered "human life". Their arguments are based on when the foetus can be said to have "personhood rights". This includes the idea, for example, that a foetus doesn't have sentience and can't think for itself, therefore it cannot be accorded the basic rights and freedoms of all human beings. The most extreme of these views is that the moment of birth grants the baby personhood rights and at such time the baby's right to life is granted. But the right to life is a negative one, and can't be granted by other humans who sit in judgment about whether a being has reached high enough levels of sentience or self-sufficiency.

The waters then get muddied even further trying to make sense of the rights of people who have lost their mental faculties or are in a coma. Does their lack of sentience mean they no longer have a right to life? Not according to some; the difference is that these people *were* sentient, they have lived lives and have people who care about them.

The difference in their situation and that of the foetus's comes down to flimsy and difficult to define concepts about what constitutes a valid human existence. How does the person in the coma have a greater right to life than a foetus just because they've had experiences and human relationships? You could argue the opposite is true, that the foetus has a greater right because they haven't yet had the chance to experience life. Of course the argument is nonsensical. By virtue of their existence both have as much right to life as the other; their current state of consciousness is irrelevant.

The problem with the idea of granting rights upon birth is that premature babies, being as they are outside of the uterus, are accorded a right to exist but a baby in utero, even at a later stage of development, is not. Within this framework a doctor can recommend and carry out an abortion at 24 weeks on one day, and then strive to save the life of a premature baby born at 24 weeks on another. The only difference in these two scenarios is the viewpoints and attitudes of the adults involved. The foetus and baby are at the same stage of development, the only difference being that the one in utero has no "personhood" rights, while other is fully human. The rights of the mother to bodily autonomy trump the rights of the unborn to exist.

Religious belief embraces a morality that is rooted in the idea that life is intended, precious and fulfils a purpose. It is upon this foundation that the moral edict "thou shalt not kill" is based. Most people, the non-religious included, would agree that murder is wrong and yet they may have trouble explaining upon what basis. Without the underlying concept that life is precious and exists for a reason the idea that murder is wrong is based on little more than personal belief.

Pro-choice people will often argue that the idea that a foetus has rights or represents human life is just an opinion, a "personal belief" of the anti-abortionist that shouldn't be imposed on others. They will flippantly say "if you don't agree with abortion, don't have one" while ignoring the fact that their own idea that "murder is wrong" (or any other social taboo) is not based on any deeper a foundation. How ridiculous it would be to say "if you don't agree with murder, then don't commit one" and advocate for the freedom of the individual to commit murder if they choose?

If you accept that a foetus is human life, then the only moral stance you can take is that abortion is wrong. It becomes very difficult to accept the common idea that abortion is a matter of personal choice, just as society would not accept that infanticide or paedophilia is a personal choice and nobody else's business. Just as infanticide and paedophilia impinge on rights of babies and children to freedom from harm, the "personal choice" of abortion is impinging on the rights of unborn humans to exist. Abortion is not victimless, and as such those opposed to abortion are driven to speak out.

Dismissing a human embryo as a "clump of cells" ignores the complex and fascinating reality that a small number of cells is rapidly dividing according to an inbuilt blueprint of development in which individual cells differentiate and group themselves according to function. The embryo and even the zygote is not a "potential human" but a "human with potential" if allowed to continue the process of development. We all started this way and these early days are undeniably a part of the entirety of our existence. If an embryo is aborted then without a doubt a human existence with all its untapped potential, is snuffed out.

Philosophical discussions about when a human life is said to begin are murky territory. They rely on arbitrary interpretations of what "life" means to construct a moral framework in which dispensing of a developing human being is acceptable. To arrive at the pro-abortion stance you must embrace the idea that although a foetus is objectively alive and developing it's not really "life". Or that it is indeed "life" but it doesn't have "personhood" or "rights" because it can't feel, can't think, can't survive on its own. You end up in a place where a headline like "Why Science Can't Say When a Baby's Life Begins" makes any kind of sense.[10]

It is well worth noting that for many pregnant women seeking abortions, there is no doubt in their minds that they are carrying a new life that has inherent moral worth. They acknowledge that their choice may be an immoral one, but to them the pregnancy is intolerable and risky, and so they put their own lives first. What is of most importance then is to seek to alter the material circumstances that make pregnancy intolerable to women in the first place and to make the case for the benefits of not aborting.

3

What is an abortion?

Most people have a strong opinion on abortion and from this we can assume that most people know what an abortion is. In the very simplest of terms it is the intentional ending of a pregnancy by removing the developing new human life from within the mother.

Because of the sensitivity surrounding the topic of abortion, descriptions that refer to foetuses or to killing are euphemised away; the most widely used definitions refer to the "termination of a pregnancy". It is quite accurate to say that a pregnancy is "terminated" when an abortion is carried out, but it does ignore the central act, which is to physically remove and thereby destroy the cells and tissues that comprise the embryo or foetus depending on the stage of development reached at the time the abortion is carried out.

The common use of the word abortion does not include miscarriage, even though medical terminology sometimes describes miscarriages as spontaneous abortions. For clarity when abortions are referred to in this book miscarriages are not included. Miscarriages occur mostly because of problems with foetal development or because of incompetencies in the cervix or uterine lining. Likewise, many fertilised eggs do not attach to the uterine wall and are passed unnoticed with the next menstrual period.

Miscarriages are rightly seen as serious and upsetting for the mother no matter how early they occur. Medical staff are sympathetic and helpful even when miscarriages occur as early as 7 or 8 weeks because they realise that for an expectant mother who wants a baby a miscarriage is devastating and is often accompanied by heavy bleeding and hormonal upheaval. Friends and family often rally around the grieving parents because they recognise that a miscarriage is a traumatic event.

Sometimes the occurrence of miscarriages is used in support of abortions because "nature does it too". Following this logic, because miscarriages sometimes happen, it is then acceptable to destroy a healthy developing foetus on purpose. This argument is comparable to saying that because cancer exists, then it's OK to murder somebody. After all nature does it too!

Abortion may sometimes be referred to as feticide, which is technically correct as feticide is the act of killing a foetus. In the US, the *Unborn Victims of Violence Act 2004* means that feticide is a homicide if the foetus was killed during the enactment of any Federal crime. In the Act, the foetus is defined as "a member of the species *Homo sapiens*, at any stage of development, who is carried in the womb." The Act though, includes a provision that excludes abortions carried out with the consent of the mother. A foetus then is accorded protection from harm under the law *except* if the mother decides that the foetus is unwanted. According to the law in the US an abortion is not feticide.

Miscarriage and the *Unborn Victims of Violence Act* both serve to highlight the arbitrary way unborn embryos and foetuses are either valued by society or dismissed as dispensable depending on the attitude and feelings of the mother towards her pregnancy. For some people the feelings of mother are all that matters.

Abortion Procedures

Abortions procedures vary and are determined by the gestational age of the embryo or foetus. All abortion procedures have side effects and risks of complications. The further along the pregnancy has progressed, the greater the risk.

Medical Abortions

Medical abortions are performed in the first trimester and involve the mother taking a combination of drugs that will induce an abortion. In Australia, a combination of mifepristone and misoprostol is used. These medications are approved for use only up until 9 weeks gestation.[11] Mifepristone works by blocking the production of progesterone which is needed to sustain pregnancy, which leads to the embryo or foetus detaching from the wall of the uterus and causes the cervix to soften and dilate. Misoprostol also softens the cervix and induces uterine contractions, expelling the foetus.

The procedure includes an examination, blood tests and an ultrasound. Side effects include cramping, bleeding, nausea, headaches, fever and chills. Bleeding and spotting usually continues for up to 16 days, however, one in twelve women will experience excessive bleeding for 30 days or more. 5% of medical abortion procedures fail and must be followed up by a surgical procedure.[12]

Dilation and Curettage (suction aspiration)

This is a surgical procedure performed in the first trimester from 5 to 13 weeks gestation. The cervix is dilated with metal rods or medication and a suction catheter is inserted into the uterus to extract the growing foetus. The uterine lining is then scraped with a curette to remove any remaining tissue.

Risk factors associated with a D&C abortion include damage to the cervix and uterus, complications in future pregnancies[13], and serious infections from incomplete abortions. As with all abortion procedures, D&C abortions are associated with higher risks of mental health problems.[14]

Dilation and Evacuation

This procedure is performed in the second trimester, up to 24 weeks gestation. It involves dilating the cervix, removing the amniotic fluid then using suction and forceps to break the foetus apart into smaller pieces so they can be drawn through the cervical opening. The process is described as follows by former abortionist Dr Anthony Levatino in testimony before a US Congressional Committee:

> A second trimester D&E abortion is a blind procedure. The baby can be in any orientation or position inside the uterus. Picture yourself reaching in with the Sopher clamp and grasping anything you can. At twenty weeks gestation, the uterus is thin and soft so be careful not to perforate or puncture the walls. Once you have grasped something inside, squeeze on the clamp to set the jaws and pull hard – really hard. You feel something let go and out pops a fully formed leg about 4 to 5 inches long. Reach in again and grasp whatever you can. Set the jaw and pull really hard once again and out pops an arm about the same length. Reach in again and again with that clamp and tear out the spine, intestines, heart and lungs.[15]

Alternatively, a suction curette is applied to the foetus's chest and the heart, lungs and abdominal contents are sucked out causing instant death. The rest of the body parts are then removed using a clamp. The head is difficult to remove as is roughly the size of a large plum and must be crushed with the clamp so that it will pass out of the cervix. The uterus is then scraped with a curette and suctioned to ensure that all the foetal remains and placenta have been removed. Sometimes substances are injected in the amniotic sac or into the foetus's heart to cause the death of foetus before commencement of this procedure, so that the tissues are more pliable and easier to remove, but usually the foetus is suctioned or pulled apart while still alive. After the extraction, all the removed pieces must be examined by the abortion provider to ensure that no pieces have been left in the uterus, which could cause a serious infection.

Side effects of a dilation and evacuation abortion are bleeding and cramping, and risk factors include, among others, damage to the uterus and cervix, blood clots, infection, and placenta praevia in future pregnancies.[16]

Intact dilation and extraction (partial birth abortion)

The intact dilation and extraction abortion, sometimes known as the partial birth or D&X abortion, is like the dilation and extraction method, with the exception that the foetus is removed intact. There is no cranial compression or dismemberment of the foetus inside the uterus, instead the foetus is positioned so that it comes out of the vagina feet first. Once the body is outside the vagina with the head still inside, almost at the point of live birth, scissors are introduced into the base of the skull, then a tube is inserted to suck out the foetus's brains. The dead foetus is then delivered.

The side effects of an intact dilation and extraction are bleeding and cramping. The risks from the procedure include cervical and uterine damage, headaches, infection, PTSD[17] , toxic shock syndrome, placenta praevia in future pregnancies, pulmonary embolism and death.[18]

Partial birth abortions were outlawed in the US after the *Partial Birth Abortion Act 2003*. During the controversy over the introduction of the Act and the subsequent appeals to the Supreme Court, many claims were made in the media that partial birth abortions were only performed in extremely rare cases of severe congenital abnormality, for situations when the parents require a viewing of the body, and when the mother's life was in danger. It was also claimed by pro-abortion lobbyists that partial birth abortions only numbered in the hundreds per year.

The truth is somewhat different. In 1997 Ron Fitzsimmons, the executive director of the National Coalition of Abortion Providers admitted that he had lied in previous interviews claiming that partial birth abortions were rare. He also admitted that the "vast majority" of partial birth abortions were performed on healthy mothers and healthy foetuses at greater than 20 weeks gestation.[19]

Induction Abortion

An induction abortion is a non-surgical abortion performed in the second and third trimester, most usually after 25 weeks. The woman's cervix is dilated, and labour is induced with pharmaceuticals. The foetus is killed in utero using a solution of saline or potassium chloride which is injected into the amniotic sac. The foetus sucks the amniotic fluid with the saline or potassium solution into their lungs which burns them, as well as burning the foetus's skin, resulting in its death. The mother undergoes labour to expel the dead foetus.

Sometimes a foetus will survive this procedure and be born alive. There are many reported cases of aborted babies born alive that are either killed or left to die in the abortion facility[20] or taken to hospitals where no attempts are made to save them which is often disturbing to abortion clinic and hospital staff. In abortion clinics, methods used to kill live aborted babies include, puncturing with sharp instruments, breaking of the spine, asphyxiation or lethal injection.[21]

How many babies are born alive after this procedure? It was

revealed by the Queensland Minister for Health, Cameron Dick, that in 2015 in Queensland alone, 27 babies were born alive and allowed to die amounting to one live birth after abortion every two weeks.[22] A study conducted by the *British Journal of Obstetrics and Gynaecology* found that one in thirty abortions performed after 16 weeks result in a born alive baby, and after 23 weeks the figure reaches 9.7%.[23] In the US, many babies born alive after a failed induction abortion, have been resuscitated and survived, some them now publicly advocating against abortion.[24]

The side effects of an induction abortion include nausea, vomiting, diarrhoea, labour pain, bleeding and cramping. The risks to the mother from the procedure include incomplete abortion requiring surgical intervention, damage to the cervix or uterine lining, PTSD[25] and infection.[26]

We may never know the extent to which late-term abortions, either D&X's or induction abortions are performed on healthy mothers and babies as statistics on late term abortions are often concealed, but reports of wide-spread practice of late-term abortions certainly cast doubts on assurances by pro-choice lobbyists that these procedures are rare.[27]

Studies conducted to determine the reasons women choose abortion reveal that women who choose abortions at 20 weeks gestation or greater do so for largely the same reasons as women who abort in the first trimester, that is, concerns over finances, education, relationships and parenting challenges.[28] Seemingly late term abortions are *not* performed for life-saving reasons or severe foetal abnormality in many cases.

To many late term abortion procedures are disturbing and it's obvious why; the later the gestation the closer the foetus becomes to a new-born baby and society recognises that killing a new-born is ethically wrong. The procedures involve violent acts of poisoning, dismemberment and destruction. And yet the organism is the same entity from the very earliest stages of gestation to the latest. Killing a 6-week-old embryo results in the death of a human with potential, to the same degree as the killing of an eight-month-old foetus or a one-year old baby.

4

First do no harm

The bioethical principle of non-maleficence dictates that medical professionals should "first do no harm". Abortion procedures which inflict fatal harm on foetuses are often justified as a health benefit to the mother such as when the mother's life is threatened, or in the case of a pregnancy because of rape. Arguments in favour of legal abortion also point to the dangers of "back alley" illegal abortion and claim that legal abortions are safe for pregnant women. In advocating for abortion as a health and safety measure the adverse impacts of abortion on women are ignored, as well as the health and safety of the unborn.

Saving the Mother's Life

Abortions performed to save a mother's life are exceedingly rare. If a mother's life is in imminent danger the aim of any surgery performed is to save the mother and the foetus if possible. Some late term abortions are performed due to severe foetal abnormalities and amount to mercy killings to end the potential suffering of the new born.

Removing the foetus from the mother at a late stage of pregnancy for the sake of the mother's health, is carried out with the intention of preserving the life of the mother *and* the baby. If the baby subsequently dies this is not an abortion, which involves the intentional killing of the foetus before it is removed.

In the early stages of pregnancy the most common procedure performed to preserve the life of mother at the expense of the foetus is to remove an ectopic pregnancy. In an ectopic pregnancy the zygote mistakenly embeds outside of the uterus, most commonly in the fallopian tube, but can also implant elsewhere in the abdominal cavity. In these instances the accepted treatment is surgical removal of the zygote before the fallopian tube ruptures and it is widely accepted that rupture of the fallopian tube puts the life of the mother at risk. There would be very few pro-life advocates who would not agree that a woman's life ought to be protected by surgical intervention in these cases.

Some sources however dispute that ectopic and abdominal pregnancies are necessarily fatal to the mother or the foetus.[29] They argue that maternal death rates are lower than is commonly understood. It's very hard to argue though that a woman's life should be put at risk to see if the foetus will successfully develop in the abdominal cavity. Some doctors have proposed trying to implant an ectopic pregnancy into the uterus, and this procedure has been successfully carried out in at least two instances.[30] The current stance though is to avoid the more serious surgical procedure of implantation of the embryo in the uterus to lower overall maternal morbidity.[31] Perhaps future medical technology breakthroughs will allow for the removal and safer transplant of ectopic embryos into the mother's uterus or into a new host mother or artificial womb.

It may in some very rare circumstances be necessary to perform an abortion to save the life of a mother, but because this sometimes happens it doesn't follow that abortions that are performed for less serious reasons are justified or that they should be acceptable by society.

"Back Alley" Abortions

Another reason given for legal abortions is that women will seek abortions even if they are illegal, resulting in adverse outcomes from botched "back alley" procedures. In the US it has even been claimed that tens of thousands of women were dying before access to "safe" legal abortions. The truth is that deaths from illegal abortions were very much lower than these estimated figures. Dr Bernard Nathanson was a co-founder of the National Abortion Rights Actions League (NARAL).[32] In the 1970s he changed his mind and became an abortion opponent openly admitting that the abortion lobby purposefully exaggerated the number of deaths from illegal abortion.

> We claimed that between five and ten thousand women a year died of botched abortions. The actual figure was closer to 200 to 300 and we also claimed that there were a million illegal abortions a year in the United States and the actual figure was close to 200,000. So, we were guilty of massive deception.

In 1960 in the US it was estimated that 90% of illegal abortions were performed, not by back alley butchers with knitting needles, but by doctors.[33] The push to legalise abortion procedures was as much to do with protecting doctors from legal action, as it was for protecting women. Even though the number of deaths from illegal abortions has been exaggerated they have occurred at the hands of trained physicians which only serves to illustrate that no abortion is 100% safe, legal or otherwise.

Figures from the Centre for Disease Control show that from the period 1973 - 2012 there have been 496 reported maternal deaths from abortion procedures. 56 are attributed to illegal abortions, while 427 have occurred because of a legal abortion (13 unknown).[34] Before *Roe v. Wade*, maternal deaths from illegal abortion were dramatically declining, mainly due the availability of antibiotics. Although the rates of death from abortion procedures reported by the CDC are low overall, these figures illustrate that there *are* risks associated with abortion and that legalising it has not removed these risks.

Genetic abnormalities and trait selection

Some second and third term abortions are performed in the case of severe foetal abnormalities that will most likely result in the death of the baby. There is a case to be made that these kinds of abortions reduce suffering of both the malformed foetus and the mother who would find carrying a baby that will die in utero or within a few days of birth excruciating. Some women prefer to let nature takes its course while others prefer to abort these babies as soon as a diagnosis has been made.

There are other kinds of deformities and disorders though that mean the baby has a chance of survival and can lead full and productive life. Trisomy 21 or Downs Syndrome is one such disorder, however in Australia 95% of Downs Syndrome babies are aborted. Now that a blood test can detect Downs at 10 weeks there are fears by some, in particular parents of Downs Syndrome children, that this will lead to an even higher rate of abortion and an extinction of Downs Syndrome babies altogether, especially in light of the fact that mothers who receive a positive DS diagnoses are often pressured by medical staff to have an abortion.[35]

Some babies are aborted for even more benign conditions such as harelip and clubfoot and even because they are the wrong sex. In the future with even more genes identified that may be responsible for certain characteristics like sexual orientation or various aptitudes, there is potential for even more abortions occurring on discriminatory bases. If as a society we accept that abortions can be procured with no justification, based simply on the desires of the mother, then there is no recourse to prevent babies being dispensed of because of minor imperfections or due to "undesirable" traits.

Rape

Many people argue for unrestricted access to abortion on the basis that some women fall pregnant after being raped. Rape is a crime and tragedy and there is no doubt that falling pregnant as the result of a rape is a dreadful circumstance for any woman to find herself in. Often those in the pro-abortion camp will point to this circumstance an example of the presumed heartlessness of pro-life people, that they would wish a victim of rape to be forced to carry her rapist's child. Abortion is presented as a "cure" for the rape and assumes that aborting the baby will help the mother recover from her traumatic experience.

The truth is that not all victims of rape who fall pregnant seek abortions and estimates on the numbers of pregnant rape victims who choose not to abort their babies varies from around 30%[36] to 70%[37]. Although the woman is the victim, the baby is an innocent third party and many women who find themselves in this situation recognise this. Testimonies from women who have had abortions after rape show that an abortion does not necessarily make things better for the mother and can in fact increase her suffering.[38]

In *Victims and Victors: Speaking Out about Their Pregnancies, Abortions, and Children Resulting from Sexual Assault* the stories of 200 women who were pregnant after rape or incest are told. These stories reveal that most of these women did not seek abortions, and of those who did, many were further traumatised by the experience:[39]

> They say abortion is the easy way out, the best thing for everyone, but they are wrong. It has been over 15 years, and I still suffer.
>
> --"Rebecca Morris"

> Often, I cry. Cry because I could not stop the attacks. Cry because my daughter is dead. And I cry because it still hurts." --Edith Young

> I, having lived through rape, and having raised a child "conceived in rape," feel personally assaulted and insulted every time I hear that abortion should be legal for rape and incest. I feel that we're being used to further the abortion issue, even though we've not been asked to tell our side of the story." --Kathleen DeZeeuw

Another factor to consider is that the normalisation and societal acceptance of abortion may also make a rape victim feel pressure to have an abortion, even if her natural instincts are to keep her baby. Well-meaning family and friends may believe that an abortion will be best for her, but without any evidence that this is true. Easy access to abortion combined with outside pressures will make having an abortion an all too easy fix that sadly is often not the case.

Abortions performed due to rape represent less than 1% of all abortions.[40] They are an example of the abortion "hard cases" and highlight how the rights of the mother and foetus are in direct opposition if the mother wishes to abort. If a pro-choice person is presented with the compromise position of legal abortions for rape victims but nobody else, they will mostly reject it. This is because rape is mainly used as a justification for abortion for all women in all circumstances. The principle of necessity dictates that if a woman is severely traumatised by carrying a rapist's baby then she should be able to access an abortion, however the existence of these hard cases does not make the case for free access to abortion for less serious reasons.

Medical Malpractice

In 2006 Dr Suman Sood was found guilty of carrying out an unlawful abortion in New South Wales.[41] In this case Dr Sood gave a woman an abortion drug at 23 weeks gestation, without counselling her patient and without any evidence that she held a genuine and honest opinion that her patient would be at risk of serious danger to her physical or mental health, as per the law in New South Wales. In this tragic case, the 23-week-old baby was born in a toilet bowl. The ambulance officer who attended testified that that the baby was blue when he rescued it from the toilet but was seen to take gasping breaths in the hospital. A heartbeat was detected, and the baby turned pink, but no further attempts were made to resuscitate it as medical staff believed the baby wouldn't survive.

The baby was then given to the mother to hold until it turned blue again, at which time it was pronounced dead. The charges against Dr Sood were performing an illegal abortion and manslaughter of a premature baby, however she was found not guilty of the manslaughter charge, as bizarrely the court could not determine that the baby was alive after it had been born. Dr Sood was given a two-year good behaviour bond and was barred from practising medicine for ten years.

This case only went to court because of restrictive abortion law in NSW. If such an incident had occurred in Victoria, there would be no case to answer, as abortions can be performed without justification up to 24 weeks. It may be argued that a woman in Victoria seeking an abortion at 23 weeks would be able to freely access a "safer" abortion than the one received by the woman described above at a specialised clinic. She would not have to undergo such a horrific experience as giving birth to a premature baby in a toilet bowl gasping for breath, but instead would be able to access a surgical termination. But consider what this means: a 23-week-old foetus being surgically dismembered or burned alive with a saline solution. Surely an abandonment of the "do no harm" principle.

Abortion Impacts

The current discourse on abortion, paints it as a simple procedure that women should have the right to acquire on demand. It is described as a right, something that empowers and frees women, as well as being a safe and straight-forward procedure. Little time is spent on the negative impacts of abortion and the detrimental physiological and psychological effects it can have on women quite apart from the destruction it causes the foetus.

Physical

Like any medical procedure abortions carry health risks. Pro-choice people often point to an American study that shows that women are 14x more likely to die after giving birth than they are after an abortion procedure, however the methodology of this study has been extensively criticised.[42] The study failed to accurately link records of women who have had abortions and women who have given birth to their death certificates, using only reported deaths from both causes, which is unreliable. Studies in Finland that used record linkage methodology have shown that 94% of deaths associated with abortion are missed when only relying only on reported mortality rates.

Studies that employ record linkage methodology have found significantly higher rates of mortality after abortion, than after birth. A Danish study from 2013 that employed record linkage methodology found that mortality rates were three times higher for women who had an abortion or a miscarriage compared to those who had given birth. Not only that, the risk of death increases with the number of abortions. Women who have given birth were also found to have decreased mortality rates compared to women who had never been pregnant.[43]

Other studies conducted in California in 2002[44], and in Finland in 1997[45] and 2004[46] that use medical record linkage methodology, all demonstrate that maternal mortality rates are lower for women who have given birth than for women who have had an abortion.

Physical risk factors of having an abortion differ depending on the abortion method used. Possible complications include uterine rupture, uterine and cervical scarring, serious infection, and possible complications in future pregnancies.

Psychological

Measuring the psychological impacts of abortion is difficult given the diversity and complexity of women and differences in how they react to having an abortion. One study in *The Australia and New Zealand Journal of Psychiatry* conducted in 2013 found having an abortion is associated with "small to moderate increases in risks of some mental health problems."[47] Late term abortions may understandably predispose women to post traumatic stress disorder symptoms. A study conducted in 2010 found that not only are women who procure late term abortions susceptible to PSTD symptoms, but they are even more likely to experience them if their abortion was for social, over medical, reasons.[48]

A report by the Taskforce on Mental Health and Abortion in the US that analysed the research into the psychological effects of abortion found that "among adult women who have an unplanned pregnancy the relative risk of mental health problems is no greater if they have a single elective first-trimester abortion than if they deliver that pregnancy." However, the report also went on to say that "global statements about the psychological impact of abortion on women can be misleading."[49]

Abortion is at times painted as a benign procedure that helps and not harms women. If measuring the psychological effects of abortion on women is difficult to quantify, then we owe it to women and young girls to be honest about that. Abortion, even early term abortion, can be traumatic for many women and often doesn't solve any of the problems associated with having an unwanted pregnancy.

Ex-abortion workers and providers

It's not just the women obtaining abortions who are adversely affected. There are numerous accounts of abortion providers and clinic workers resigning from their positions after witnessing disturbing and upsetting things during the course of their work.

Doctor Bernard Nathanson was an obstetrician-gynaecologist who helped to start the National Association for the Repeal of Abortion Laws (NARAL) in 1969. At the Center for Reproductive and Sexual Health, an abortion clinic in New York that he established in 1970, he presided over 60,000 abortions. By the mid 1970s he began to be "deeply troubled", especially after development of ultrasound technology allowed him to clearly observe the foetus.[50] By the end of the 1970s he'd stopped performing abortions all together and started campaigning against them. In 1985 he was featured in *The Silent Scream* in which he narrates over a recording of an abortion enacted on a 12-week-old foetus.[51]

Anthony Levatino is another former abortion provider who is now an active pro-life campaigner. In his training to become an obstetrician and gynaecologist performing suction abortions was part of his weekly routine, as well as occasional later term procedures that involved injecting saline into the amniotic sac and which resulted in whole foetuses being expelled sometimes still alive. After he and his wife had trouble conceiving he became very conflicted about all the pregnancies that he was helping to terminate. He also felt the contradiction that came with celebrating the heartbeat of a 7 or

8-week-old foetus with its parents during an ultrasound appointment, while a couple of hours later aborting foetuses at the same or later stages of development.[52] His website features details and risk factors of various abortion procedures in the hope that women will be swayed from choosing one.[53]

Abbey Johnson is one of many former abortion clinic workers who have become pro-life after witnessing harrowing events while performing their clinic duties. As a clinic director for Planned Parenthood, she soon realised that instead of performing abortions as an "unfortunate necessity", clinics were selling a product and a profitable one at that. After assisting with an ultra-sound guided abortion of a 13-week-old foetus, she realised that she could no longer support abortion and sought help to not only leave her position with Planned Parenthood, but to expose the abortion industry's shortcomings.[54] In 2016 she along with co-author Kristin Detrow published *The Walls are Talking*, a collection of stories from former abortion clinic workers in which they anonymously detail their harrowing and life changing experiences.[55]

Abortion is neither the harmless nor simple procedure that it is made out to be by abortion supporters. As with any medical or surgical procedure there are risks that include serious infection, permanent damage to the cervix and uterus, the possibility of complications in future pregnancies and death. In addition there are no mental health benefits to obtaining an abortion over proceeding with an unwanted pregnancy. Women are being sold a bogus ideal when abortion is presented as a right and a liberation. We deserve better!

Abortion Survivors

Not all abortions are successful. Failed abortions are another negative impact of abortion that is ignored by pro-choice activists.

Some aborted foetuses somehow survive the procedure and are born alive after which they are granted personhood status. Unsurprisingly many of these abortion survivors have become vocal anti-abortion activists and campaign and against abortion in the hope of changing social attitudes.

There are two main types of abortion survivors: people who survived the abortion procedure that was carried out on them and people who were twins in utero and their twin was aborted. Both are traumatising experiences. Imagine living with the knowledge that you were unwanted enough by your mother that she tried to abort you, and yet because the procedure failed you have had a chance to develop your consciousness and are now fully aware of it.

Claire Culwell only found out in her adult life that she was an abortion survivor.[56] On finding her birth mother she was informed that she'd had an abortion aged 13 years old. After still showing signs of pregnancy it was discovered that she had been pregnant with twins and the abortion had only removed one foetus. She now campaigns actively to educate pregnant women on alternatives to abortion.

Melissa Ohden found out at the age of 14 that her birth mother actually went through a saline abortion procedure at 5 months gestation. She had been left in the procedure room but then the nurses noticed she was still alive. Miraculously she suffered no physical effects from the saline solution which usually works by scalding the foetus's skin and lungs. After finding out about her survival she was devastated, and her first reaction was one of anger, but she soon moved to a place where she found she could forgive her parents. She has dedicated her life to speaking out against abortion.[57]

Josiah Presley is a young Korean man whose mother sought an abortion when she was two months pregnant. Later she realised she was still pregnant but decided to proceed with the pregnancy and adopted him out to an American family after he was born. He has a deformed arm from the failed abortion. Josiah campaigns actively against abortion and believes that all unwanted babies would be adopted especially if adoptions were made more affordable and more easily accessible.[58]

These are just a few of the many stories of people who survived abortion procedures. The overwhelming takeaway from these stories is that abortion survivors see life as a precious gift. The people they are now began their lives as "clumps of cells" which contained within them all the potential that is now fulfilled in their adult lives. Judging a developing foetus as disposable simply because it isn't capable of feeling pain or thought processes is discarding something of inherently supreme value based on its current status. A foetus *will* develop in to a human being if allowed, and as such is of immeasurable value to other human beings. Every year over 55 million human beings worldwide are aborted and with them the value that 55 million human lives brings.

5

Abortion and the law

Abortion law in Australia rightly remains the jurisdiction of the states. Each state has their own legislation which ranges on a scale of highly restricted abortions with elements in place to protect both the right to life of the unborn and pregnant women based on the principle of necessity; and fully legal abortion at the discretion of the mother. Let's have a closer look at the law in each jurisdiction.

NSW

Abortions in NSW and Norfolk Island are unlawful under sections 82-84 of the *Crimes Act 1900 (NSW)*. The interpretation of the law is based on the ruling by Justice Levine in R *v. Wald* (1971) which stipulates that an abortion is legal if a doctor believes that there exists "any economic, social or medical ground or reason" an abortion is required to "preserve the woman involved from serious danger to her life or physical or mental health which the continuance of the pregnancy would entail". In other words, abortions are illegal unless the wellbeing of the mother is at stake.

In theory, abortion law in NSW protects both the right to life of the unborn as well as the rights of pregnant women to appropriate care, however abortions in NSW can be procured effectively on demand by making the case that the mother's mental health would be adversely affected by continuing the pregnancy, a subjective condition that is open to a broad interpretation. Doctors must make the appropriate investigations, however, before referring a woman for an abortion, and if they do not they are at risk of prosecution.

Recently Greens MLC Mehreen Faruqi introduced the *Abortion Law Reform Bill 2016* into the NSW state parliament which would have made abortion legal up until birth, required doctors who object to abortion to refer their patients on, and enforced a 150-metre buffer zone around abortion clinics. After heavy campaigning by pro-life advocates, a parliamentary petition against the bill was tabled with 56,559 signatures, and the bill was voted down by the Legislative Council in May 2017.

Queensland

Abortion law in Queensland is similar to that in NSW and is governed by the *Criminal Code Act 1899 (QLD)*. Abortions are illegal at any stage unless deemed medically necessary to protect the mother. Because of the similarities to the law in NSW, the circumstances under which abortion is permitted are determined are based on the same case law, that is 'only in exceptional cases will abortions be deemed lawful'.[59]

South Australia

In South Australia abortions are governed by the *Criminal Law Consolidation Act 1935*. The law is similar to the law in NSW and Queensland in that abortions are illegal unless deemed medically necessary. A woman must have resided in South Australia for at least two months to procure an abortion.

Northern Territory

The *Termination of Pregnancy Law Reform Act 2017* makes abortion legal in the Northern Territory. A woman can obtain an abortion up to 14 weeks after being assessed by one doctor, and between 14 and 23 weeks after being assessed by two doctors. After 23 weeks abortions are only legal if required to save the mother's life. The only criminal provision is that an abortion provider be suitably qualified.

Tasmania

Under the *Reproductive Health Act 2013* abortions in Tasmania are legal. A woman can attend an abortion clinic without a referral and receive an abortion up until 16 weeks. After 16 weeks, abortions are still legal, but two doctors must agree that the termination is "appropriate".

Western Australia

In 1998 the *Criminal Code 1913* and the *Health Act 1911* were amended to make it legal to obtain an abortion up to 20 weeks gestation subject to suitable counselling. Beyond 20 weeks abortions can only be performed if the unborn child has a severe medical condition and they must be approved by two independent medical practitioners in an approved facility. If the mother is under 16 years of age, a parent must be notified.

Victoria

Abortion law in Victoria before the *Abortion Law Reform Act 2008* was similar to the law in NSW and Queensland. Abortions were illegal but available through the application of the principle of necessity.

The reform act now allows for abortions on request up to 24 weeks. Beyond 24 weeks abortions are still legal up until birth provided two doctors agree that it is "appropriate, based on the woman's current and future physical, psychological and social circumstances". The only criminal provision is that abortion providers must be qualified.

ACT

Reference to abortions in the *Crimes Act 1900* were repealed in 2002, making abortions legal on demand up until birth with no medical justification required. Abortions in the ACT are now regulated in the same way a standard medical procedure might be. Furthermore, the Territory's *Human Rights Act 2004* explicitly denies an unborn baby any right to life claiming that this right commences from birth.

Patrick Ferdinands in his comprehensive paper in *Deakin Law Review*, outlines the case for safeguarding the rights of the unborn in the law, based on the principle of value.[60] The potential value of an unborn person, that is their future value to other human beings, should be considered when weighing up the rights of the mother to bodily autonomy versus the rights of the unborn foetus to life.

It is clear that abortion law in Australia varies wildly between restrictions based on necessity and no restrictions at all. Where there are restrictions in place, increasing value is placed on the foetus the further developed it is. Any measurement of the value or worth of the unborn child is currently based on the stage of development and ignores their potential future value to society. For example, under Northern Territory law abortion is freely available to a woman in the early stages of pregnancy up to 16 weeks, then between 16 and 23 weeks two doctors must agree to it, and after 23 weeks an abortion is only available if medically necessary. The further along the foetus is developed, the more consideration must be given by the mother and her doctor.

A 4-week-old embryo has future value equal to a ninth month old foetus. References in the law to the stages of development of a foetus when determining their worth reflect perhaps the common view that more developed foetuses are more human and thus less easily disposed of. This may reveal an ignorance of foetal development especially considering new developments and discoveries in the fields of embryology that show that foetuses and embryos show startling levels of complexity at the very earliest stages.

Additionally, in Australian law the unborn only become a legal person once born alive. This is a legal fiction designated so that legal rules can be applied. It is not based on science, or on any great philosophical truths about humanity or morality but rather it represents a point in time from which certain laws can be said to apply. For example, if a baby was injured in the womb, there is no basis for separate charges related to the baby's injuries unless the baby is born alive, at which point it becomes a "legal person," and charges can then be laid against a perpetrator based on the injuries received by the now born baby. Despite this, the death of a foetus is viewed as an aggravating factor in sentencing, so the presence of the foetus is not entirely discounted if injuries suffered by the mother result in its death.

In 2009 Brodie Donegan's unborn daughter Zoe was stillborn after Brodie was hit by a drug affected driver while walking.[61] The driver was only given a 9-month term as the judge could not fully account for the death of Brodie's child under the law. As previously noted, damages to an unborn baby 'crystallise' legally at the point that the baby is born alive. If the baby is stillborn, as Zoe was, then it has no legal protection. Upset with the lenient sentence, Brodie began working with Liberal MP Chris Spence to introduce a bill dubbed 'Zoe's Law' which sought to grant legal status to the unborn. Although the bill passed the NSW lower house, it languished in the upper house after opposition from pro-abortion advocates who rightly foresaw threats to abortion rights once the unborn had legal protection. The bill eventually lapsed.

Although on the surface Zoe's Law seemed to be pro-life, it was inconsistent. This is demonstrated by the cut-off point of 20 weeks (or 400 grams). This arbitrary point of development could have serious implications for any perpetrators involved in an incident that causes the death of an unborn baby. One day or a few grams difference would result in vastly different outcomes for all involved.

Another inconsistency was that the legislation exempted any medical procedure, or any action done with the consent of the woman involved. In other words, the unborn would have been granted personhood status only if harmed by anyone other than its mother or by medical personnel during a medical procedure. If a pregnant mother was to drive recklessly and accidently kill her unborn baby, then the law would not apply; if any other driver was at fault, then the unborn baby's legal status would be upgraded.

The main problem with abortion law in Australia is that it does not properly safeguard the rights of both women and unborn children.[62] In no jurisdiction are the unborn granted legal personhood. Also the existence of pro-choice legislation in Victoria, WA, the NT, Tasmania and the ACT undermines the law in the other more restricted jurisdictions. Not only can women easily circumvent the law in NSW and QLD for example by travelling interstate to procure an abortion, any convictions of abortion providers leads to outrage and comparisons to the more liberal laws in the less restricted states.

Abortion law that allows for abortions upon request right up to birth, such as abortion law in the ACT, also fails to protect women who are at risk of coercion. Women who feel pressure to have an abortion from partners or their social networks can often defend their decision to keep their baby because it is now "too late". A woman in the ACT is not afforded that protection, and can could potentially face coercion up until the point of birth.

Conversely pregnant women who face health or psychological risks proceeding with their pregnancy also need to be able to trust that they are protected under the law and not forced to carry a pregnancy that will adversely affect their health. Good abortion law will recognise that abortions may sometimes be required, but also that abortion should only take place for serious reasons.

When discussing abortion law, it is important to acknowledge that if abortions are illegal, women will face penalties of some sort. Most pro-life people would agree that women ought not to be punished to the same degree as a person who has committed wilful murder. Nobody wants to see women locked away for seeking abortions and yet at the same time if a foetus is recognised as a human life worthy of protection then the law must enact a punishment of some sort. There is no simple answer to such a wicked problem, however it is reasonably consistent to be pro-life and seek to legal protection for the unborn while at the same time not wishing to see women incarcerated for making such a choice.

Evictionism

Walter Block's theory of evictionism is an idea that tries to deal with the moral dilemma of abortion based on the libertarian principle of property rights.[63] Evictionism recognises that the unborn is a human existence from conception, but paradoxically supports the woman's right to evict a foetus for any reason. The mother is viewed as a property owner (her body) and the foetus, a trespasser. The mother has the right to "evict" the foetus as gently as possible if she no longer wants to carry it, but not to explicitly kill it. Within the evictionist legal framework, a woman has no right to an abortion when there exists an option for the foetus to survive outside of the uterus.

The current state of medical technology means that most evictions from the uterus, no matter how gentle, would be fatal to the foetus. Only a very few foetuses at certain stages of development could survive an eviction. Evictionists however, look to the future to a time when medical technology would allow the removal of a foetus from a woman's body unharmed, so that it can continue to develop in either a new host mother or in an artificial womb. Such technology may not be very far away.[64]

Eviction theory recognises the value of a developing human life; it doesn't try and arbitrarily pinpoint a time at which a foetus becomes "life" or achieves "personhood". It is opposed to the radical feminist idea that a woman has the right to kill a foetus at any stage of its development and its author Walter Block describes abortion as an "evil". Evictionism recognises that destroying a foetus in utero is wrong and draws a line between killing a foetus (an abortion) and evicting it from a woman's body, even if the result of the eviction is that the foetus dies. It denies any obligation of the mother to keep the foetus alive by carrying it.

This stance offers up a compromise between the pro-life and pro-choice positions and recognises that the unborn are helpless victims of abortion. However, it is based entirely on property rights and legality and sets aside questions of morality. It still does not solve the dilemma of the deaths that occur when a mother evicts. If it can be said that abortion is immoral, then how much more moral is eviction if it mostly results as it would at the current level of medical technological development with the death of the foetus?

Block does make the point though that even at current levels of medical technology, a foetus evicted in the ninth month, or even the eighth month would have a very good chance at survival. If anti-abortionists campaigned for eviction legislation and were successful it would result in at least some otherwise aborted foetuses being saved. It would mean, however, letting go of any position that requires a woman to carry a foetus to term against her wishes. It also creates a minefield of ethical dilemmas around how evicted foetuses would be treated and there would have to be assurances in place to protect such babies from being unnecessarily institutionalised.

Although evictionism does not yet present a viable third way it is worthy of serious consideration. Once medicine has developed a way of keeping evicted zygotes, embryos and foetuses alive to be adopted by people who are willing to take on the care and responsibility of a human baby then pro-abortion arguments based solely on the bodily autonomy of the mother become null and void. Within a future evictionist legal framework a woman would be able to make decision about whether she wants to carry a foetus to term but she would not have the power to grant or deny the foetus life itself.

Unfortunately, emerging research on artificial wombs already has some pro-abortion people worried. Their arguments are that a woman not only has the right to not be pregnant but that she also has the right to no genetic off-spring, or in other words the "right not to procreate.[65] " Even the evictionist framework is not enough to satisfy those who demand the right to kill their foetus.

6

Free to Choose

The biggest argument for abortions is based on the woman's right to her bodily autonomy. We are told that a woman's right to choose trumps the right of a developing baby. In truth, even without abortions a woman has the power to make choices that give her the ability to steer her life in the direction of her choosing. She can choose her partner, whether to marry, her career pathways, her contraception.

When it comes to reproduction, a woman's first choice is whether or not to have sex. We all know that having sex is not just an enjoyable experience, it also comes with a certain amount of risk. But for most women who do not want to get pregnant, abstinence is unrealistic. Fortunately, in the modern era woman have a choice of options that prevent conception, and that are easy to access, cheap and effective. Most of the time, if used correctly, contraception is highly effective. But if it fails, then the resulting pregnancy is a natural consequence of engaging in voluntary sex. Freedom is the ability to make choices, but with freedom comes responsibility for the consequences of our own actions even if we don't like them.

The overwhelming reasons why women choose abortion are not for the "hard" cases that used to argue for legal abortion like rape, incest or health problems. The most cited reasons are "not ready to have a baby right now" (74%) and "can't afford a baby right now" (73%). 48% cite relationship problems, and 38% say they've finished with childrearing. Only 1% of women cite rape as a reason and less than .5% are due to incest.[66]

Most abortions are being performed because for some women, their pregnancy is intolerable. But abortion presents a wicked problem where there is more than just the woman's body to consider. Another human being's life is at stake.

Abortion and Feminism

Most feminists, with some exceptions, are supportive of abortion rights as they believe abortions emancipate women from reproductive slavery. Abortion rights, it is argued, give women autonomy over their bodies and the power to end a pregnancy that is unplanned or unwanted. Ultimately pregnant women have the final say over whether their baby will live or die. Slogans such us "my body, my choice", and "stay out of my uterus" reflect this thinking.

There are some feminists however who argue that abortion harms women more than it helps them. The earliest feminists were against abortion and viewed it as exploitation of women and children. Their focus was on addressing the root causes that lead women to want abortions. American suffragist Victoria Claflin Woodhull said of abortion:

> Many women who would be shocked at the very thought of killing their children after birth, deliberately destroy them previously... The truth of the matter is that it is just as much a murder to destroy life in its embryotic condition, as it is to destroy it after the fully developed form is attained, for it is the self-same life that is taken.[67]

Instead of freeing women abortion allows society to continue not to cater for the needs of mothers. Granting ready access to abortion means the state can spend less on childcare support, employers can more easily ignore the flexibility needs of women in the workplace and men can expect access to sex from women with less concern for their obligations should she fall pregnant.

When society is accepting of abortion then women are also more susceptible to coercion. Consider a young woman who finds herself with an unintended pregnancy. Her boyfriend is keen for her to have an abortion, and she knows her parents will not be happy that she is pregnant. Even if she would rather keep her baby, the combined pressure from her partner, her own desire to maintain the approval of her parents, and the dominant social view that says that abortions are acceptable and women-friendly, may mean that she has an abortion because she feels that she "should".

Jaya Taki former girlfriend of National Rugby League star Tim Simona, revealed how she felt pressured into having an abortion. After finding out that Jaya was pregnant, Simona told her that having a baby would ruin his rugby league career. He ignored her unless she was willing to talk about making an abortion appointment. After the abortion, she struggled to live with her decision and experienced ongoing suicidal tendencies. She spoke in NSW Parliament House against proposed legislation that would see abortions legally available up until birth for any reason.[68]

Another high-profile incident in 2016 involved rugby league player Bryce Cartwright. After finding out his girlfriend was three months pregnant he informed her that he wanted nothing to do with the pregnancy. She eventually succumbed to persistent pressure from Cartwright and another man and obtained an abortion after being paid $50,000 to do so.[69] Afterwards she took her story to the media. In both of these cases women were pressured into having abortions they didn't want by men who sought to avoid the natural consequences of their own behaviour. Freely available abortion then helps to mask the symptoms of societal dysfunction often to the detriment of women.

Some pro-life feminists also argue that abortion violates feminist principles of anti-violence and non-discrimination. This idea is expressed in a position statement by the group Feminists for Life: "We believe in a woman's right to control her body, and she deserves this right no matter where she lives, even if she is still living inside her mother's womb."[70] Bodily autonomy is important, and that includes the bodily autonomy of unborn babies.

Even though abortion is claimed as a right and championed by most modern feminists, rates of abortion are thankfully going down and even pro-choice advocates celebrate these statistics. The main reason cited for lower rates of abortion is increased access to, and more reliable contraception,[71] although in the US only 62% of women of reproductive age use contraception and so this doesn't fully explain the trend. Another proposed reason for the decline is the increased social acceptance of single motherhood which has reduced the stigma associated with getting pregnant outside of marriage.

Victoria Woodhull dreamed of a day when women, freed from the restrictions imposed on them by the society of the 1800s and early 1900s, would no longer be required to resort to abortion:

> Is there, then, no remedy for all this bad state of things? None, I solemnly believe; none, by means of repression and law. I believe there is no other remedy possible but freedom in the social sphere... Freedom is a great panacea. It will be when women are thrown more on their own resources, when they mingle on more equal terms with men, when they are aroused to enterprise and developed in their intellects; when, in a word, a new sort of life is devised through freedom, that we can recover the lost ground

of virtue, coupled with the advantages of the more advanced age.

Sadly, as yet, the "advantages of the more advanced age" such as financial freedom and access to contraception have not yet resulted in us achieving the "lost ground of virtue" to which Victoria Woodhull refers. To reduce abortion rates even further we need to seriously examine the reasons less women are choosing abortion and seek to change the circumstances that lead women to believe that an abortion is in their best interests.

Adoption

Adoption is an obvious choice for pregnant women who don't want to keep their babies and for couples and families who either cannot have children or desire to give unwanted babies and children a loving home. Unfortunately, in Australia adoption is often a long drawn out and expensive procedure. A September 2017 report *Barriers to Adoption* issued by Adopt Change, an organisation committed to transforming attitudes and laws about adoption in Australia, has found that Australia has large numbers of prospective adoptive parents but that over 80% of them find the adoption processes complex and overwhelming. Less than a third of adoptive parents feel supported by the adoption agencies with which they are dealing.

Additionally, 83% of prospective adoptive parents have faced barriers to adoption including marathon amounts of waiting time. For over 40% of adoptive parents the adoption process took over 5 years. These barriers are often highly personal and unjustified including, for example, prospective parents being turned away for having too high a Body Mass Index! The result of all these restrictions and hurdles is that only 196 children were adopted in 2016 down 5% from the previous year: the lowest number on record.

There are indications in some states that open adoption processes are being actively explored. That there are large numbers of prospective adoptive parents willing to go through the current arduous processes, proves that these people are committed to the welfare of children. Unfortunately, because of forced adoptions in the past adoption in Australia is sometimes seen as socially unacceptable.[72] If adoption taboos can be broken, and procedural reform enacted, then adoption can become a realistic option for women with unwanted pregnancies.

We deserve better

In the *Roe v. Wade* ruling the supposed detrimental effects of a woman unable to obtain an abortion were listed as psychological harm, lack of child-care, the trauma of being an unwed mother, the mental and physical health of the mother, the economic resources of the mother and the mother's ability to care for the child. As discussed previously, abortion simply masks the root causes of these effects by merely eradicating the symptom. Social change that more fully supports women, including access to affordable childcare, social safety nets and employer flexibility, already has and will continue to go a long way towards reducing these impacts. Adoption reform that allows women to adopt out unwanted babies in a non-judgmental and fully supportive environment, as well as cutting red-tape and reducing costs for adopting families will also reduce the impacts of unplanned and unwanted pregnancies on women.

Of course, many women choose abortions unapologetically. They don't claim to be escaping psychological harm or financial burden or coercion. They simply don't want to be pregnant. This is a sad indictment of the legal and social acceptance of abortion which has some women believing that ending their pregnancy is moral choice available to them free of consequences. Victoria Woodhull's hopes for regaining the "lost ground of virtue" are yet to materialise. Abortion harms women, harms men, harms medical professionals and harms unborn babies; we all deserve better.

7

Abortion arguments

A zygote, embryo or foetus isn't a human being

If they are not human then what are they? Dogs, monkeys? The words zygote, embryo and foetus do not describe a "thing" but rather they are descriptive of a stage of development. Human zygote, human foetus, human baby, human toddler. A zygote, embryo or foetus are humans at very early stages of development. They are human beings, and as such are entitled to all the protections that are inferred by universal human rights.

Some people liken a zygote to sperm cells or skin cells. They say things like: "a sperm is life, where do you stop?" But what sets zygotes apart from other living cells in our bodies, is that a zygote is a unique new human life with its own DNA made up of the combination of the haploid sperm cell of the father and the haploid egg cell of the mother. It lives, grows and develops, unlike a single sperm.

In abortion debates, people sometimes say that science can't really pinpoint when a human life begins. And yet this ambiguity doesn't apply when we talk about non-human reproduction. You don't hear scientists or veterinarians saying that they're not sure at what stage a new chicken is made, they know very accurately when this happens. Likewise, an IVF scientist knows the exact point at which a human life is created in the laboratory. Separated from the emotion that often surrounds abortion debates, science is clear about when a new human life is created.

A foetus is not a person

Claims that human foetuses are not alive or not human are unscientific. Because of this arguments for abortion often turn to philosophy. Philosophical arguments as to the personhood status of unborn humans need only be based on personal beliefs about what it means to be a human person and such beliefs can be used to support the idea that killing unborn humans is ethical.

For some people a human is not a person until they are born. Up until that point the unborn human being is not a person in any legal sense and can therefore be denied human rights and consequently any right to life. This means that a foetus can be killed at the discretion of the mother right up until the point of birth. Others choose more arbitrary points during gestation at which a foetus can be deemed a person such as the point at which a heartbeat is detected, or the brain has developed, or when the foetus can feel pain, or "viability". These determinations are discriminatory. Humans deserve human rights because of what they are (human), not what stage of development that are at (foetus, baby, toddler).

Some arguments base personhood on the ability of a human being to be rational, sentient and self-aware. On this basis, a zygote is not seen as a person because it has none of those attributes, like a bacterium or a simple life-form. Unlike bacteria though, a zygote doesn't have those attributes simply because it hasn't had time to develop its brain. Its very nature is to develop a brain and gain sentience. A single celled life form never will.

What then of the new-born baby, or the person in a coma? Are they to be denied personhood status because they are not rational and self-aware? Once again, a human being is deserving of human rights because they are human, because of their nature, not because of their ability or their rationality.

Arbitrarily assigned personhood rights represent a two-tiered model of humanity: those that have human rights, and those that have them denied by others. History is replete with people being denied the status of personhood including black people, the disabled, homosexuals and Jews. Denying personhood status to unborn human beings is a philosophical device to justify killing them out of convenience. The right to life is an unalienable right that can't be bestowed by or withdrawn by others as it suits their purposes.

Abortions are OK before the foetus is viable

The foetal viability argument says that a foetus is not a person with human rights because it is so dependent on its mother that it couldn't survive outside the womb. Before the point of viability, a foetus can be dispensed with. This line of reasoning means that the more vulnerable the human foetus is, the less it is protected. One of the basic tenets of civilised society is that we protect the most vulnerable. That is why women and children have traditionally been the first to be rescued in crisis situations, and why we have child protection laws. Surely the more dependent on the mother the foetus is, then the more responsible we are to protect it.

My Body, My Choice

Even if we grant human rights and personhood status to foetuses, there remains the dilemma of the moral and bodily autonomy of the mother. Clearly there is a clash of rights, and somebody's rights must give way. The mother's right to bodily autonomy must be weighed up against the foetus's right to an existence. What is of the greater importance, a human being's right to an existence, or a woman's right to control what is happening inside her own body? If the mother carries the baby to term, both can live; if the mother has an abortion then only she survives.

Often then the pro-choice person will fall back on the personhood argument so that the rights of the mother to bodily autonomy can be seen as more important than the life of the non-person, non-human being that is the foetus. If there is no "person" being killed by an abortion, then of course the mother's rights are all that matters. As we have seen though, denying personhood rights to the unborn is arbitrary.

If a woman wants to kill her children because she can't afford to take care of them or she finds it hard, would we encourage her to do it? No, we would help her with other options. What if she was to turn around and say, you're forcing me to have a hard life with these children." Would it make any sense? Arguing that denying abortion to women is forcing them to carry a baby to term is dishonest and implies aggression and violence when the opposite is true. The pro-life position is that killing unborn babies is wrong, and it is the abortion that is forceful and aggressive.

A woman's right to control her body and make choices about her reproductive status is a very real right that pro-life people support. Where they draw the line though, is at taking another person's life, and there can be no denying that when an abortion occurs a human life is lost.

The foetus is a trespasser

Some pro-choice people claim to be evictionists. They believe that an unwanted pregnancy means that the foetus is trespassing on the mother's uterus, and that she is within her rights to "evict" the trespasser from her property. This idea is akin to kidnapping someone in a coma, dragging them onto to a plane with you, and when you decide you don't want them on board anymore, throwing them out at 12,000 feet. This would not be a moral thing to do, even if you own the plane and no longer desire to have your passenger on board. Even though the person is unconscious and unaware that you are throwing them out of the plane to their death, we recognise that it would be the wrong thing to do. In such a case the property rights of the plane owner defer to the property rights of the unconscious passenger over their own body and life.

The foetus cannot "trespass"; it is powerless and has been brought into existence by its mother and father. It is not the aggressor, but rather has had life thrust upon it by the actions of its parents. The obligation then of the mother is to act justly towards the foetus and to not initiate lethal aggression through the act of eviction.

The hope of the original proponents of the eviction framework was to potentially save the lives of foetuses that would otherwise be aborted once medical technology has advanced enough to keep evicted foetuses alive. Recent advances in artificial wombs however have already been met with opposition from some pro-choice people who argue for not only a women's right to bodily autonomy but also for the right to not procreate. This means even evictions and artificial wombs are not enough to rescue unwanted foetuses in the face of demands for the right to no genetic offspring, that is the right to a dead foetus.

Every child a wanted child

Some pro-choice people claim that abortion helps to combat poverty and saves children from being born into bad situations. But a poverty-stricken life is better than no life at all. Not to believe so is to think that people in poverty would rather be dead. Additionally, non-white people are overrepresented in low socio-economic groups especially in the US. Advocating abortion to solve poverty equates to aborting more African-American babies and reducing the African-American population proportionately. It is unbelievably paternalistic to claim that unplanned or "unwanted" babies would be better off dead and ignores the fact that a great many successful people had less than ideal childhoods.

If the testimony of abortion survivors is anything to go by, these supposed "unwanted" babies are very much wanted by their own selves. Ask any "unwanted" child if they would rather be alive or dead and you can almost guarantee that most of them would choose life. These unwanted and unexpected unborn babies already exist and it's too late now to say that they'd be better off not existing. What greater example of privilege can there be than the claim that only wanted or well-off babies deserve life. Suffering is part and parcel of the human condition. If avoidance of future suffering is the justification for aborting unwanted babies, then we may as well abort all babies.

There are very many families that are willing and able to adopt unwanted babies if only adoption was less socially taboo and more readily accessible. In a world that allowed free and streamlined adoption processes, unwanted babies would have access to all the opportunities that planned for babies enjoy.

Women will do it anyway

It is true that there has always been a market for abortions. The best approach then is to seek to understand why women want them, and to try and remedy the social conditions that lead them to view abortion as their only option. The real aim of the pro-life movement is to make abortion a less desirable choice than the other options open to women.

The dominant cultural view is that abortion is a legitimate moral choice available to women backed up by beliefs that the unborn are not human beings or persons. When society accepts this premise then abortion is used flippantly as form of birth control backup evidenced by the statistics that show that most abortions are undertaken because the mother isn't "ready to have a baby" or "can't afford a baby right now."

Other factors such as social shame lead women to seek abortions and this is complicated by conservative outlooks that frown on unwed mothers instead of supporting them. Recently a pregnant teen at a Christian school in the US was barred from graduating with her class-mates.[73] This kind of punitive reaction is part of the problem that sees young women in particular, ending their pregnancies.

Even so, just because women may seek abortions regardless, it doesn't justify their legality. We don't say "people will steal cares anyway, so we may as well make it legal" or "murder happens anyway, so let's make it safer for murderers to exercise their choice." The big question to ask is, is it OK to sanction the killing of unborn babies, because some people want to do it?

Legal, Safe and Rare

In 1996 Bill Clinton coined the term "legal, safe and rare" in reference to abortion. The slogan was intended to soften the impact of the Democrat's support for legal abortion on people who were unsure or uneasy about the issue. The argument for legal abortion is that legal abortion is safe and that by making abortions legal they will be safe, legal and rare. The truth is that like any medical procedure, abortion is not 100% safe, and therefore we shouldn't trivialise it. As discussed there are very many negative physiological and psychological impacts of abortion on women. Also, abortions are not rare. According to the Guttmacher Institute during 2010-2014 56 million abortions were performed world-wide each year.[74] The promised ideal of legal, safe and rare abortions hasn't materialised. Instead abortions are legal, commonplace and have negative physiological and psychological impacts that are often ignored. What needs to change is societal dysfunction and the abortion culture that sees abortions as a solution rather than a symptom.

Pro-lifers are really just pro-birth

That idea that people who are pro-life don't care about women or babies is a claim often made but never substantiated. People sometimes say, if you're pro-life and don't adopt children then you're a hypocrite. But this is an unfair and inaccurate claim to make, on a par with suggesting that humanitarians are hypocrites if they don't house a family of refugees. As we have already discussed, there are plenty of people who would willingly adopt unwanted babies, but adoption procedures are often prohibitive. It also ignores the work many pro-life people do volunteering their time to offer pregnancy support and counselling.

Another accusation often made is that pro-life people, Christians in particular, are hypocrites because they also support the death penalty. This ignores that abortions are performed on innocent human beings, whereas the death penalty is meted out only for serious crimes, and so holding that position is not necessarily incoherent. But even so, US surveys show that Christians who support the death penalty are in the minority.[75] Indeed the Roman Catholic Church, the most outspoken Christian denomination against abortion, also supports a pro-life position on the death penalty and indeed against violent forms of protest against abortion:

> If anyone has an urge to kill someone at an abortion clinic, they should shoot me. ...It's madness. It discredits the right-to-life movement. Murder is murder. It's madness. You cannot prevent killing by killing. ~ John Cardinal O'Connor

People who support a pro-life position on abortion are diverse in their political opinions and have different views on a range of political issues. There are pro-life atheists, pro-life Christians, pro-life conservatives and pro-life progressives. Comparing the views of pro-life people with their views on other political issues is just "what-about-ism", a logical fallacy that accuses a person of hypocrisy while at the same time avoiding refuting any of the arguments being made.

Abortion empowers women

Abortion is detrimental to women and allows society to treat the symptom rather than the cause of societal dysfunction. Rather than addressing economic inequalities and the devaluation of life and motherhood, it's easier to promote abortion to make the problem go away. Abortion allows society to continue to neglect to cater for the needs of women and sets women up to be coerced into abortions they may not want to have. It allows men to access women for sex with less concern for their obligations. Social acceptance of abortion gives women less power to say no.

Don't like abortion? Don't have one

Would we say the same thing about murder or paedophilia? Don't like paedophilia? Then don't practise it! Just don't try and force your views onto other people who want to be paedophiles! Of course, this argument is ridiculous. Paedophilia is harmful to children and encroaches on their rights to live free from aggression and the freedom of adults to practise it must be restricted. Just like abortion.

I'm personally pro-life, but politically pro-choice

This argument is very similar to the one above. When a pro-life person recognises that an unborn baby is a human being and a person and therefore killing them in-utero is morally wrong, then it is incumbent on them to oppose abortion. It's not enough to say, "I wouldn't do it myself." Abortion is about more than the personal choices of women. It involves the fate of the youngest and most vulnerable members of society that we should all care about protecting.

8

Changing Attitudes

It's true that making abortion illegal will lead to women obtaining abortions anyway. This is because to many women, their pregnancy is intolerable to them and they wish to end it, even with the full knowledge that what they are doing is an immoral choice. Others believe it *is* a moral choice, and a right. This then presents us with the challenge of changing society so that women will no longer want abortions. We can make a start by reducing the stigma of single motherhood and adoption, promoting policies that support mothers in education and the workplace, educating the women who may not know that their foetus is more than a mere "clump of cells", and continuing to speak out about the reality of abortion procedures and their adverse effects.

Many women have been hoodwinked into believing that abortion is safe and morally acceptable, without having been given the full story of what an abortion is, how it is performed and the inherent risks of the procedure. Abortion procedures aren't widely discussed, and photos of aborted foetuses are "graphic" and deemed to be unacceptable and overly emotional.

Many women have been duped by a society that accepts abortion as an expression of the moral autonomy of women, that says that they are exercising their "rights" to bodily autonomy without any acknowledgement at all of the bodily autonomy of the foetus. They are told that abortion helps women, while ignoring the thousands of women who have been adversely affected by abortion.

People who advocate for abortion rights expect that women ought to be free to transcend their very nature, even if that involves the killing of another human being. It speaks to a mind-set that elevates a woman's right to make choices about her reproductive life above the right of another human being to an existence. In the 21st century, greater numbers of women have more autonomy than ever before. They have the right to choose their career path and their partners. They have a range of contraceptive methods from which to choose, if they do not wish to become pregnant. They have the knowledge that the sex act may result in the creation of a new human being, and they have the autonomy that allows them to choose to have sex or to abstain.

Yes, contraception does fail sometimes, but personal responsibility dictates that when the unexpected happens, then we deal with the cards that we are dealt. To kill another human being just because their existence is an inconvenience, is a moral failing.

If we can change our collective attitude toward abortion such that pregnancies are valued, and women are given appropriate support, then women may be less likely to think of abortions as a valid option. To paraphrase the Abortion Abolitionists, there is one thing that is worse than abortion, and that is the worldview that makes it acceptable in the first place.

Let's change our world so that abortions become unthinkable.

Let's stop using pretzel logic that pretends that foetuses aren't alive or human or persons.

Let's recognise the gravity of abortion.

Let's stop absolving ourselves of responsibility by saying that it's just a matter of the mother's choice. Would we respect a mother's choice to kill her new-born baby?

Let's acknowledge that abortions carry health risks that are both psychological and physical.

Let's fix adoption law to make adopting unwanted babies easier.

Let's stop being an "abortion culture" that embraces the harmful ideology of "abortion without apology" and that accepts abortion as a contraception backstop.

Women who seek abortions are victims of circumstance. Let's aim for a cultural change that rejects the killing of foetuses and supports women to make choices that respect the dignity of human life and their own.

Endnotes

1   Psalm 139:1, 13, 15, 16 (ESV).

2   R. C. Sproul, *Abortion: A Rational Look at an Emotional Issue* (Orlando: Reformation Trust, 2010); Peter Barnes, *Abortion* (Edinburgh: Banner of Truth Trust, 2010).

3   "Abortion," *Gallup*

4   Norman M. Ford, "When Did I Begin?: Conception of the Human Individual in History, Philosophy and Science", *Cambridge University Press*, 1991.

5   "The Fetal Senses: A Classical View", *World Organisation of Prenatal Education Associations*, February 20, 2016.

6   Rajender Bhatia, "15 Stories Of Premature Babies That Survived Against The Odds," *BabyGaga*, November 12, 2016.

7   Viola Marx and Emese Nagy, "Fetal Behavioural Responses to Maternal Voice and Touch," *PLOS ONE* 10, no. 6 June 8, 2015.

8   V. Schöpf et al., "Watching the Fetal Brain at Rest,'" *International Journal of Developmental Neuroscience* 30, no. 1, February 1, 2012.

9   "When is the Foetus 'Alive'?", *BBC Ethics Guide*.

10   Zhang Sarah, "Why Science Can't Say When a Baby's Life Begins," *WIRED*, October 2, 2015.

11   "Medication Abortion", *Children by Choice Association Incorporated*, July 4, 2016.

12   "Abortion Pills", *Abortion Procedures: What You Need to Know*.

13   Jennifer Lohmann-Bigelow et al., "Does Dilation and Curettage Affect Future Pregnancy Outcomes?", *The Ochsner Journal* 7, 2007.

14   David M. Fergusson, L. John Horwood, and Joseph M. Boden, "Does Abortion Reduce the Mental Health Risks of Unwanted or Unintended Pregnancy? A Re-Appraisal of the Evidence," *The Australian and New Zealand Journal of Psychiatry*, September 2013.

15   "Doctor Who Did 1,200 Abortions Tells Congress to Ban Them," *LifeNews.com*, May 23, 2013.

16   "Second Trimester Abortions", *A Woman's Right to Know*.

17   Priscilla K. Coleman, Catherine T. Coyle, and Vincent M. Rue, "Late-Term

Elective Abortion and Susceptibility to Posttraumatic Stress Symptoms," *Journal of Pregnancy*, June 28, 2010.

[18] "Abortion Procedures," *A Woman's Right to Know.*

[19] David Stout, "An Abortion Rights Advocate Says He Lied About Procedure," *The New York Times*, February 26, 1997.

[20] Sarah Terzo, "Abortion Workers Admit Infants Who Survive Abortions Are Killed Outside the Womb," *Live Action News*, June 8, 2016.

[21] "The Human Rights of Babies Surviving Late Abortion," *European Center for Law and Justice*, February 17, 2014.

[22] Crystal Jones, "27 Qld Babies Born Alive after Failed Abortions, Left to Die," *News Mail*, June 14, 2016.

[23] "The Human Rights of Babies Surviving Late Abortion," *European Center for Law and Justice*, February 17, 2014.

[24] *The Abortion Survivors Network.*

[25] Priscilla K. Coleman, Catherine T. Coyle, and Vincent M. Rue, "Late-Term Elective Abortion and Susceptibility to Posttraumatic Stress Symptoms," *Journal of Pregnancy*, June 28, 2010.

[26] "Abortion by Labor Induction," *A Woman's Right to Know.*

[27] "The Human Rights of Babies Surviving Late Abortion," *European Center for Law and Justice*, February 17, 2014.

[28] Lawrence B. Finer, Lori F. Frohwirth, Lindsay A. Dauphinee, Susheela Singh and Ann M. Moor, "Reasons U.S. Women Have Abortions: Quantitative and Qualitative Perspectives," *Perspectives on Sexual and Reproductive Health*, 2005.

[29] B. Fortenberry, "Ectopic Personhood," *The Personhood Initiative*, March 11, 2015.

[30] L. Shettles, "Tubal Embryo Successfully Transplanted in Utero," *American Journal of Obstetrics and Gynecology* 1990. C. J. Wallace, "Transplantation of Ectopic Pregnancy from Fallopian Tube to Cavity of Uterus," *Surgery, Gynecology, and Obstetrics*, 1917.

[31] J. Balasch and P. N. Barri, "Treatment of Ectopic Pregnancy: The New Gynaecological Dilemma," *Human Reproduction (Oxford, England)*, March 1994.

[32] William Grimes, "B. N. Nathanson, 84, Dies; Changed Sides on Abortion," *The New York Times*, February 21, 2011.

[33] Mary Steichen Calderone, "Illegal Abortion as a Public Health Problem," *American Journal of Public Health and the Nations Health*, July 1, 1960.

34 Jatlaoui TC, Ewing A, Mandel MG, et al. "Abortion Surveillance — United States, 2013," *MMWR Centers for Disease Control and Prevention*, November 25, 2016.

35 Barbara Miller, "Parents Feel Pressured to Terminate Pregnancy after Down Syndrome Diagnosis," *ABC News*, November 22, 2016.

36 M. M. Holmes et al., "Rape-Related Pregnancy: Estimates and Descriptive Characteristics from a National Sample of Women," *American Journal of Obstetrics and Gynecology* August 1996.

37 David C. Reardon, "Rape, Incest, and Abortion: Searching Beyond the Myths," *The Post-Abortion Review*, 1994.

38 David M. Fergusson, L. John Horwood, and Joseph M. Boden, "Does Abortion Reduce the Mental Health Risks of Unwanted or Unintended Pregnancy? A Re-Appraisal of the Evidence," *The Australian and New Zealand Journal of Psychiatry*, September 2013.

39 Makimaa, Sobie Reardon, "Victims and Victors: Speaking Out About Their Pregnancies, Abortions, and Children Resulting from Sexual Assault," *Acorn Publishing*, 2000.

40 Julia Medew, "Report Reveals Abortion Reasons," *The Sydney Morning Herald*, January 19, 2009.

41 Geesche Jacobsen, "Doctor Guilty of Illegal Abortion," *The Sydney Morning Herald*, August 23, 2006.

42 Elizabeth G. Raymond and David A. Grimes, "The Comparative Safety of Legal Induced Abortion and Childbirth in the United States.," *Obstetrics and Gynecology*, January 31, 2012.

43 Priscilla K. Coleman, David C. Reardon, and Byron C. Calhoun, "Reproductive History Patterns and Long-Term Mortality Rates: A Danish, Population-Based Record Linkage Study," *European Journal of Public*, August 1, 2013.

44 David C. Reardon et al., "Deaths Associated with Pregnancy Outcome: A Record Linkage Study of Low Income Women," *Southern Medical Journal*, August 2002.

45 M. Gissler et al., "Pregnancy-Associated Deaths in Finland 1987-1994--Definition Problems and Benefits of Record Linkage," *Acta Obstetricia Et Gynecologica Scandinavica*, 1997.

46 Mika Gissler et al., "Pregnancy-Associated Mortality after Birth, Spontaneous Abortion, or Induced Abortion in Finland, 1987-2000," *American Journal of Obstetrics and Gynecology*, February 2004.

[47] David M. Fergusson, L. John Horwood, and Joseph M. Boden, "Does Abortion Reduce the Mental Health Risks of Unwanted or Unintended Pregnancy? A Re-Appraisal of the Evidence," *The Australian and New Zealand Journal of Psychiatry*, September 2013.

[48] Priscilla K. Coleman, Catherine T. Coyle, and Vincent M. Rue, "Late-Term Elective Abortion and Susceptibility to Posttraumatic Stress Symptoms," *Journal of Pregnancy*, June 28, 2010.

[49] "Mental Health and Abortion Task Force Report," *American Psychological Association*, August 2008.

[50] Bernard N. Nathanson, "Deeper into Abortion," *New England Journal of Medicine*, November 28, 1974.

[51] "The Silent Scream," *American Portrait Films*, 1984.

[52] "Dr Anthony Levantino", *Life Zone*.

[53] "D & E Abortion Procedure | What You Need to Know," *AbortionProcedures. com*.

[54] "About Abby," *Abby Johnson.org*.

[55] Abby Johnson and Kristin Detrow, "The Walls Are Talking: Former Abortion Clinic Workers Tell Their Stories," *Ignatius Press*, 2016.

[56] Claire Culwell, "My Story," *ClaireCulwell.com*.

[57] Melissa Ohden, "The Story of a Life," *MelissaOhden.com*.

[58] Josiah Presley, "My Name is Josiah and I am an Abortion Survivor," *Abolish Human Abortion*, March 14, 2012.

[59] *R v Bayliss and Cullen (1986)*

[60] Patrick Ferdinands, "How the Criminal Law in Australia Has Failed to Promote the Right to Life for Unborn Children: A Need for Uniform Criminal Laws on Abortion Across Australia," *Deakin Law Review*, 2012.

[61] James Robertson, "'Zoe's Law' Bill Lapses Closing Controversial Chapter," *The Sydney Morning Herald*, November 20, 2014.

[62] Patrick Ferdinands, "How the Criminal Law in Australia Has Failed to Promote the Right to Life for Unborn Children: A Need for Uniform Criminal Laws on Abortion Across Australia," *Deakin Law Review*, 2012.

[63] Walter Block and Roy Whitehead, "Compromising the Uncompromisable: A Private Property Rights Approach to Resolving the Abortion Controversy," *Appalachian Journal of Law*, 2005.

[64] Emily A. Partridge et al., "An Extra-Uterine System to Physiologically Support the Extreme Premature Lamb," *Nature Communications* April 25, 2017.

[65] I. G. Cohen,"Artificial Wombs Are Coming. They Could Completely Change the Debate over Abortion," *Vox*, August 23, 2017.

[66] Lawrence B. Finer, Lori F. Frohwirth, Lindsay A. Dauphinee, Susheela Singh and Ann M. Moor, "Reasons U.S. Women Have Abortions: Quantitative and Qualitative Perspectives," *Perspectives on Sexual and Reproductive Health*, 2005.

[67] Cat Clark, "Victoria Claflin Woodhull," *Feminists for Life*.

[68] "Women Denounce Extreme Abortion Bill in Panel at Parliament House", *Youth for Life Australia*.

[69] "Bruce Cartwright allegedly involved in deal to pay woman $50,000 to have an abortion", *News.com.au*, March 6, 2017.

[70] "Arguments Against Abortion", *BBC Ethics Guide*.

[71] Emily Crockett, "The Abortion Rate Is at an All-Time Low -- and Better Birth Control Is Largely to Thank," *Vox*, January 18, 2017.

[72] Jeremy Sammut, "Unless We Break the Taboo around Adoption, Child Welfare Problems Will Continue," *The Sydney Morning Herald*, November 9, 2015.

[73] Jessica Chasmar, "Pregnant Teen Banned from Christian High School's Graduation for Being 'Immoral,'" *The Washington Times*, May 25,, 2017.

[74] "Induced Abortion Worldwide," *Guttmacher Institute*, March 2018.

[75] Jonathan Merritt, "Poll: Younger Christians less supportive of the death penalty," *Religion News Service*, January 17, 2014.

www.ingramcontent.com/pod-product-compliance
Lightning Source LLC
Chambersburg PA
CBHW031523270326
41930CB00006B/498